Global Citizen

Thinking Beyond

Nurbek Achilov

First Edition

Nurbek Achilov
Global Citizen: Thinking Beyond, 2019

1st Edition
All Rights Reserved
ISBN: 9781074306021

Table of Content

Tables

Figures

Dedication

I dedicate this handbook to my children, who are very young to understand today's world disparity and challenges, but they are forming a new thinking now and it is important to provide them with global ideas to let them bring new changes around the country and the world.

This is a special book for them to build a global mindset from small steps to actions.

They have to learn new global skills, a new way of thinking and prepare themselves for new global actions.

It is indeed complex topic and I tried to measure right angles to describe them the topics in the simplest way and from my own experience.

Introduction

For many centuries, our humanity is in the fight for land, resources and capital. Divided by more than 10 religion groups, 200 countries, thousands of languages and ethnic groups, we lost our global unity, efficiency and development.

From aside, we simply live in the world of disparities, inefficiency and constant dilemmas. In the fight for natural or financial resources, some countries are still nationalistic, some are hegemonic and the others are religious. There are many states where dictatorship is prospering. They lead their countries in the way that the right solution is the solution of the ruler, not a global community or majority about safety, common actions or development.

The today's solution is a global mindset. And we, as national citizens, have to be global citizens to take over the issues and find new solutions.

The first aim of this handbook is to uncover a new type of person – a global citizen, its mission, principles and actions. The second step is to show our challenging global and regional issues we face today and also many others, which will confront in the future. The next aim is to describe what should we do as a global citizen to resolve our regional and global issues. The last point, is to point out a number of features, which can help a global citizen to act and achieve the mission and goals.

The one interesting part of this book is to show the personal experience in Turkestan region of how I could motivate local people for global mindset and become global citizens. Turkestan region is in the heart of the Eurasian Continent and the most developed centers are far from the region.

Moreover, local citizens were in the isolation for more than 7 decades and under the propaganda of the Soviet information policy. Before Soviets, the region was under khan ships, which fought with each other for centuries even with the same ancestors. It formed the most bureaucratic and inflexible mindset of people who are still facing the difficulties, adapting to the market economy.

The idea was to motivate other readers to spread the voice of the global citizen via a handbook. With clear steps and recommendations, this book allows not only individuals, but also organizations and countries to change their understanding of the global citizen. To eliminate a fear of globalization, which many people despise in various countries, especially in those with strong national traditions, religion and single language policies.

This is also a motivation book for young people to become a global citizen in heart and in mind. The more and more global citizens can unite for global actions, we can create our unique global culture for more efficient global infrastructure and economy.

As global citizens we can achieve and do our changes uniting together and defending the future from random and venal decisions.

Who is the Global Citizen?

Global Citizen is a person with its global values and traditions, who has understanding of humankind as a single nation, with common values for living and working in our planet, without harmful effects for nature, surroundings and other people.

Today, as citizens of various countries people divided by languages, history, traditions, thinking and their national values. In many countries, people speak only their own local language with no interest to learn other tongues. These circumstances create certain barrier for communication, common actions and efficiency.

Today, we have to ask ourselves: who am I? who I want to be? An isolated person or global citizen. A nationalist, who cares about own national values and traditions, which are slowly disappearing or global citizen, who wants to find common values and advantages for development, efficiency and common actions. At the same time, global citizen understands and applies the best practices of both national and world history and culture.

Let me explain from my own experience. My interest to other cultures and economies was one of the reasons I tried to accept new principles from world leaders, red their motivating books, travelled to new destinations, organized international events, took part in a number of global activities etc. Gradually, it formed my global mindset, which helped me to look at the same processes with a totally opposite mind and generate many ideas to turn other people to a different direction. It was in areas of business, ecology, education, science, and many other areas.

I involved myself in the global institutions which actually open for everyone. For example, I am a member of Global Citizen Platform at www.globalcitizen.org, G-Global Info-Communication Platform at: www.group-global.org, Eurasian Economic Club of Scientists Association and many others. These institutions were a gateway for new ideas and formation of my global culture.

Involving and supporting various global activities and actions, communicating with people around the world and writing articles and books on global topics, I have been analyzing issues and facts based on global approaches and point of views. Step by step, I understood that I formed a totally different global culture inside me. For the same situation and fact, I was looking with an absolutely different view – an eye of Global Citizen.

It is not about a passport, which can certify about Global Citizen status or any other proved case. It is also not about Global Institutions, which you represent or where you are a member today. Till the moment, we do not have such institution that evaluates people global mindset and provide them with Global Citizenship. However, this is not a case to say that we cannot be a global citizen at all.

Living in any country of the world, with our national passport or document, we can be a true Global Citizen. The more and more Global Citizens will become first in mind, the sooner the Global Institution will be created for certification of global citizenship in near future.

So, the Global Citizen today is a person who keeps global principles, values, traditions and many other knowledges by heart and in mind, which can be seen in activities and actions a global citizen works every day.

Why we have to be the Global Citizens?

In the period of dividing our communities into countries or groups based on political views, social and economic statuses, it is hard to unite people for common actions on a global scale. That's we cannot see and take over our polluted oceans and environments in time.

Today, on a regional level, many people do not care about what they breath, eat and consume daily. Many people do not care about their health and offspring. They are isolated in many dimensions and do not care about other nations, our environment, our food supply and many other key points of human existence in future.

In many cases, their communication is limited. As they do not understand what global experts and scientists are speaking around the world about various global issues and trends. For sure, they need a single language or they a need a technology, which can instantly translate any language for understanding each other. However, even with the same language and a unique technology in place, they cannot form same values to act together. But they can communicate and gradually educate themselves to think in the same direction of the global citizens. Thus, this means that anyone can become a global citizen with proper communication and education.

We can only unite with global mindset in heart and mind. It can help us to unite our intentions and actions into a global movement. This can make our relationships stronger and powerful, especially in overcoming the most difficult issues of the regional and global agendas.

In fact, globalization is our new future and our duty to prepare people, especially, offspring to move the progress further. They have to learn how to cope with many barriers of communication, thinking, values, multiple traditions etc. They have to learn to create common values too. And it is about education.

Without being a global citizen, we cannot simply educate our children to adapt them to global trends. We cannot talk and explain them how they have to communicate with other nations.

And this book is a starting point to change and motivate our communities for new direction. It should become a handbook to start changes in mindset and create global citizens in heart.

This should also motivate globalists to write many books on specific issues, especially on Global Government and Global Citizenship, which can be accessible online to any person who passes certain criteria for global actions.

How to become a Global Citizen?

This question I asked myself decades ago, when I had a wish to study abroad and make the first contribution for economic development of the region and then of the global economy.

I was not a unique student or person; I was without any gadgets or technology or people nearby who can direct me. I can imagine now how many times this could increase my efficiency of work and intentions if I would have a laptop 20 years back, for example.

So, the interesting question is: how could I become a global citizen without any gadgets or technology, or uniqueness?

After reviewing myself and the period of changes, I defined several key factors. They are:

- Language
- Upbringing
- Education
- Principles
- Global Missions
- Global Actions

Let me briefly explain how these factors helped me to become a global citizen.

Languages

At home I speak Kazakh, at school I used to speak Russian and, in the yard, Uzbek Language. From very young age my farther taught English, for example, how to count or say greetings etc.

It helped me to receive information easily from various sources and communicate easily, on the one hand, and to build my interest in other languages, on the other.

After I entered university, I started to read professional books in English and German. My early English and multi-language character gave me so much advantages in learning and exploring new areas.

When I started my professional work, I was very interested to understand other cultures, their thinking and values. I started to learn Japanese, Chinese and other languages to succeed at work.

Generally, languages helped me to access the progressive information faster, effectively and in certain extent in wide range of topics, which were not covered in post-soviet countries.

Till the moment, I consider a language as a communication and learning tool. In fact, no other factor provides so wide access for learning cultures, traditions and many other differences we have among countries, social groups, etc.

So, the first starting point is a language. It is important to learn English Language today to access the global information sources in various fields. It is also about communication. For example, with English you can talk people almost in any country of the world.

So, the first languages to learn are:

1) English
2) French
3) German
4) Spanish
5) Arabic
6) Chinese
7) Russian

But language is not the only factor, which drives person's global mindset. For example, there are billions of people, who speak English around the world, however, they have limited understanding about the global issues, cultures and are careless about global trends and problems.

Upbringing

There are many skills, knowledges and experiences, you can only learn in your family. Family is a powerful source for supporting, motivating and developing one's character.

Your father and mother, grandparents, brothers and sisters, other relatives are contributors of your character. Only in the family, you can learn how to behave, respect, share and love. Only in the family you understand your identity, learn values and traditions and listen true stories about the past, people and ancestors.

For example, I was lucky to spend some time with my grandfather and listened his stories about Germany, France, Italy and other countries in very young age. It formed my interest and dreams about the countries, which I visited later in my life.

Further I also learned many important lessons and evaluations from my grandparents. They were the only source I could understand many mistakes of other people in learning and acting, including of my parents and other elder people around. So, it formed a certain character that I have never grown the bad habits no matter of circumstances.

Moreover, my grandfather taught me how to plant a tree in the yard, saying how important trees for bringing fruits and oxygen for people.

Abovementioned shows that we have to care about children and especially what kind of information and care they receive in their babyhood and during the school years, vacations.

Today, many children grow up in the orphanages and many with parents without basic upbringing and education about nature, people around.

The main areas for children to understand are:

1) Countries
2) Nationalities
3) Religions
4) Cultures
5) United Nations
6) Nature
7) Ecology
8) Plants
9) Animals
10)Wastes
11)People
12)Races
13) others

Number one priority in upbringing is to prepare global citizens from the young age. And build their interest for many areas of our global agenda.

Education

The next important factor is education.

If stopped my education with school or bachelor degree, I would never have a chance to become the global citizen in heart and actions.

Education helped to level up all the skills and requirements, including for English, thinking, vision, competences and other skills necessary to work in the professional way.

When it is about global knowledge, it is important to understand that anyone can become a true global citizen at any age, no matter of past life.

Life-long education is one of the solutions, which can balance human imperfections and omissions by targeted content and programs for any age group.

The priority is to evaluate the person's horizon of thinking and actions, which can fit in to the level of global actions. For example, majority of people around the world are not interested in global matters. They think that they have to resolve their social and economic issues first. And, on the other side, they believe that the global issues are far from their reality. They have to think about how to find a food for today or for their babies.

If we take from an international perspective, any local vision above is a global issue. For example, lack of food in one country can be resolved if people, who live in that country, to understand that in other countries the food is in abundance. Or a high level of poverty and unemployment in one country are pushing people to think locally, for example, to earn their daily money only. But when they are educated, they will think on many ideas and solutions how to increase their sources of income. For example, they can learn how to create the high value products and use an advantage for exporting new products, for example, via e-commerce tools.

Therefore, a number one task is to focus on life-long education and post-graduate programs which can train people at any age on how to be a global citizen.

For global citizen, it is important to build programs in the following fields:

1) Geography;
2) World History;
3) International Relations;
4) International Business;
5) Cross-Cultural Management;
6) Waste Management;
7) Strategic Management.
8) Others.

These areas of education that will form interlinks between many areas and sectors of the economies.

Principles

Upbringing and education help any person to build life-long principles. Many principles change many times, but the core ones are for whole life.

The best thing about the principles, they can change over the time based on new experiences, knowledge and circumstances.

For global citizen, it is important to build the following principles:

1) Open mind. It means that a person should be open for any new ideas to discuss, accept or think critically.
2) Global thinking – Regional application. For any issue one has to think globally and realize an idea based on people's budget, mindset and other local circumstances.
3) Self-motivation and learning skills
4) Punctuality in all matters
5) Honesty on all issues and activities
6) Fairness in decision and allocation
7) A person of word
8) Being responsible
9) Others.

The principles are the only source of human's motivation that can drive a person for knowledge on a constant base.

Global Mission

One day after listening many ideas about our global issues, especially polluted environments, drying out Aral see, ecology and oceans, I formulated my own global mission to do my best to change people's attitudes and character. My mission included a change toward nature, ecology, wastes and global issues, including financial, economic, social topics etc.

I understood that I am not the only person in the world and at least I can do my best in the country where I am living and can benefit millions of people. So, I started it from Kazakhstan and the Central Asia.

I was lucky to join the Astana Economic Forum which was an event of 100-300 participants. In few years, with global approach, we could unite more than 12 000 delegates and participants. The faith in global mission, helped me to convince many top managers and government people in the direction of the Astana Economic Forum and the internet platform, which was a connecting element of annual forums. The ideas of the internet platform were to discuss global issues on a constant base, long before participants could meet in the Astana Economic Forum. Later, thanks to the President of the country our internet platform transformed to the G-Global Info-communication Platform. Now it still runs discussions about the topics of the coming Astana Economic Forum.

This allowed us to gather recommendations and prepare the final outcomes of the forum to present them annually to the United Nations, G-20 leaders and other global institutions.

My global mission has never stopped, even after I left the organizing committee of the Astana Economic Forum.

I understood that this mission is still drives me to areas where other people and leaders have never looked at. After moving the provincial Shymkent city, my global mission helped me to uncover advantages of the region from a different angle – a global perspective.

Based on observations and analysis, I developed recommendations and reports connecting local cities such as Shymkent and Turkestan to the Great Silk Road, the past history of khan ships including the Chinggis khan and Tamerlane and also to the followers of the prophet Mahomed. I showed how important are the cities for global trade between East and West and also for global tourism, as in Mausoleum in Turkestan city, not only the Khodja Ahmed was engraved, but also more than 300 descendants of the Chinggis khan.

During the Soviet period, the vast territory of the khans was divided in the Soviet Republics. And in the near past, each ruler in the republic was thinking that he is the one who has the most power. It created many barriers between countries, especially between Kazakhstan and Uzbekistan, Uzbekistan and Tajikistan, Uzbekistan and Kyrgyzstan. I did my best to provide information for governors of the countries to change the thinking from a global perspective and from the past history.

My Global Mission helped me to see the most difficult issues of the region from the totally different angle – again a global perspective. Making our problems so tiny before the global issues which require more efforts to unite nations for common actions.

Global Actions

When a person has a limited view or have never thought on issues from global perspective, a person will act based on personal values, local traditions and hardships. No matter of the position, social status or income a person will be selfish, nationalistic or narrow-minded in many issues.

Global actions are the actions which are done based on global perspectives, issues and understanding of the outcomes for global communities. It requires a specific knowledge to act critically, absorb new ideas, lessen difficult situations and influence people in the positive way.

There are four areas where we can apply global actions: 1) personal issues 2) local issues; 3) regional issues and 4) global issues.

Let's see how we apply global actions on personal issues. First example, everyone wants to be the best specialist. If a person lives with local understanding and actions, he will probably end up in the school. But if a person acts on a personal issue with global actions, he will end up with doctoral degree or an international degree.

Second example is the job place. If a person acts locally, he will end up in the company with narrow market and scope. But if a person applies and works in the company with the global actions, his or her company will go with its products or services beyond the borders of the region, country or continent.

How to apply global actions on local issues. For example, if we take drying out Aral see with local actions we will end up with paperwork and no positive changes for local people. For example, in areas around Aral see people struggle from lack of water, salty winds and sandstorms. And no single government program can support them till now.

When we can do it with global actions on local problems of Aral see, we can demonstrate the most devasting case for the whole world, especially who are living in the cities and better climate conditions. With global actions we can draw the attention of millions of people for support and taking actions, especially in regard to local government activities and budget allocation. Global actions can push local governments to work effectively and provide support for local people in their migration or receiving their social benefits.

The same with regional and global issues. Global actions can resolve the most dangerous and ecological issues with the support of global community. For example, owners of the ships and sea boats, which throw daily millions of tons of garbage will hide their activities, which will be unnoticeable for people who live far from ports, islands, or seashores. They can only understand the problems and effects of the tankers or waste boats from people with global actions only.

Our mission for global actions has no limit in application. We can act with global actions on any issues of our community agenda. Let's see some other examples of classification of global actions.

First, regarding personal issues which can be classified as the following:

1) Providing life-long education for all;
2) Developing the products or services for multinational markets;

3) Psychological or social problems of the women or children;
4) Creating unique artworks etc.

In the regard to local issues, they include areas such as:

1) Unemployment and job creation;
2) Educating people;
3) Stability from Inflation;
4) Green Construction;
5) Home services etc.

These local issues, if resolved with global actions can be resolved easily. For example, today the unemployment issues resolved by creating a production lines under old financial schemes or technologies. The same with educating people. In many countries, universities are educating youth with specializations, which are not demanding anymore. From a global perspective, according to many international experts, more than 100 specializations will disappear in near future, but at the same time, more than 150 new specializations will be created and demanding. So, if the local government will push its new programs for creating absolutely new ventures with demanding specializations, then they will stimulate local people to learn new specializations. And it is clear that colleges and universities will follow the trend.

Regional issues are complex in terms of country driven or ethnic driven issues. From perspective of Asian or European countries, they include:

1) Drying out Aral see;
2) Annexed Crimea;
3) Uighurs in China;
4) Ukraine and Russia tensions;
5) US and China Trade War;
6) India and Pakistan tensions;
7) Afghanistan's war and peace issues;
8) Sanctions on Iran and Russia;
9) Separatism in Spain and Russia;
10) Effects of Chernobyl on East Europe;
11) Syria ethnic fight;
12) Brexit;
13) Border tensions etc.

In some way, these complex issues are limited with one or several countries and in many cases they are regional. The only problem is that they are now resolved with local and regional approaches, based on ideas and comments of local people.

From global perspective, for example, if all countries of the region will understand the effects of the drying out of the Aral see on glaciers, water resources and heath of people in Tajikistan, Kyrgyzstan, Uzbekistan and Kazakhstan, they will take different approaches in regard to agriculture, irrigation systems and water-supply systems.

In regard to Annexed Crimea is an issue of destroying the life of not Ukrainians, but according to many experts, the life of the Crimean Tatars, who cannot receive their republican status because of Stalin policy on nations, who served Hitler's Regime during World War II. But it happened more than 70 years ago. And now absolutely new generations of people are living in the peninsula and around the world.

Again, if this regional issue taken from global perspective, the issue will be resolved easily. Crimean Tatars have their ancestors from Turks, Russians, Germans and many other nations. They have no single gene, which belong to one nation. So, there is no point of doing ethnic or country policy over the Crimea for politicians. If the local people want to be independent or be in the part of one country, they have to decide themselves, not the Russia, Ukraine or Turkey or any country of the world.

Unfortunately, today, global issues are also resolved with local or regional approaches. Therefore, we have so many barriers for interconnection and common global efficiency. Nations understand and fight for land, and they are careless in regard to oceans, nature, ecology and the most terribly for the life of their people, their families and themselves, and most importantly for their offspring. That's because people evaluate the wealth of today as a possession of something. It can be a land, people, paper money or some other valuables.

What are the Global Trends and Issues?

We have to accept that many of our previous and present generations have never thought about the global trends and issues to work on them.

That's why we can see now so many wars in the past and present, drying out of Aral see, nuclear bomb tests, Chernobyl catastrophe in the Ukraine, melting of glaciers because of climate change and many other ecological outcomes.

Actually, till now, there is no clear classification of global trends and issues in full scope. Probably it is a big topic of new research for us together.

Despite that, let's try to classify our main global issues and trends below as a preliminary step:

1) Climate change;
2) Pollution of air;
3) Pollution of underwater and oceans;
4) Pollution of products;
5) Pollution of orbit;
6) Waste Land fields and Management;
7) Epidemies and healthcare;
8) GMO and other ingredients;
9) Extreme Poverty;
10) Drainage and water supply systems;
11) Food supply and systems;
12) Illegal Migration and Traffic;
13) Global Energy Networks and Sources;

14) Global Security and National Disarmament;
15) Nuclear and Radiation Security;
16) Personal Security Protection;
17) Global Financial Architecture and Currencies;
18) Global Economy and Entrepreneurship;
19) Dictatorships and Democratic Elections;
20) Global Citizenship;
21) New technologies and patents;
22) Outdated education;
23) Global Networks and Roads;
24) Human Rights;
25) Nationalism;
26) Corruption;
27) Terrorism;
28) Exploration of cosmos;
29) Exploration of earth and many other;

From a global perspective, there are many issues that require involvement of all nations in a chain of common actions. There are many platforms like Global Citizen or G-Global Info-Communication Platform, which raise and discuss the issues, call for global actions on the one side. And organizations such as United Nations, OSCE, CICA and many other organizations, on the other side. They all work on global issues and call for actions. But they are limited in terms of execution power.

From analysis, I could see several issues:

1) Power of interest. With only country interest in mind it is impossible to drive the global issues for a result.
2) Corruption. According to some experts of the UN, many programs are realized with corrupted networks of diplomats and country leaders.
3) Geopolitics. Many experts note that some leading countries want to control the countries and lands which were their colonies in the 17-19 centuries.
4) Science. Using science and development as an instrument of trade wars and controlling the markets.
5) Local thinking. Many areas and countries of the world are still blocked from internet, information access and free trade.
6) Others.

There are many platforms, where leaders of countries meet together to resolve their policies and agree on single policies for effective collaboration. However, that's not enough. There are only around 100 main global leaders around the world. And they work in their specific areas: politics, business, media etc. International relations and global collaboration are the areas where we can see not leaders, but more experts, diplomats and politicians who are working in the interest of their countries.

That's the main point, why global citizens are demanding to solve the global issues with their global actions. This is also the point why we can grow global leaders – global citizens effectively to take the most active role in different parts of the world. They can effectively understand the global trends and issues and lead their countries and nations toward common global actions.

Today we can solve our global issues as global citizens only. Global citizens are the new leaders of our global era. Only they can lead their nations to meet the challenging issues and unite for global actions.

Here, it is important also to classify two types of global trends.

First, the trends, which are consequences of human activity. For example,

-climate change,

-waste landfills,

-ocean waste,

-country specific and regional riots,

-global trade wars,

-excavation of natural resources,

-political disputes and debates,

-epidemics,

-migration,

-human rights,

-drying of rivers, lakes and sees,

-and others.

Second, global trends which are consequences of human activity, limited natural resources or technological changes. For example,

-digitalization of the countries,

-robotization of economies and industries,

-development of alternative sources of energy,

-artificial intelligence management systems,

-big data centers,

-implementation of green technologies,

-regional and global integration of transportation, logistics and other systems,

-development of global cryptocurrencies,

-integration of markets for wholesale and retail,

-exchange programs between countries,

-etc.

Global trends help us to understand new opportunities for global actions. They help global leaders where to focus, adapt and how to resolve those issues in time.

On country level, it is important that governments work on their policies integrating them with global policies. Generally, global politics is a new instrument that can accelerate the process of forming global citizens for actions and resolving global issues.

Global Politics

Many authors explain the global politics as a study to find the traits and relationships between countries for global politics.

But, actually, it is the wrong way to come to the global politics. Because, many countries build their policies and politics exceptionally based on their local interests, or interests of limited group of people to manipulate and control natural and financial resources of their countries.

That's a truth of today's politics. No matter of the size of the country or its intentions to globalize.

Global Politics, in fact, should be a foundation of the countries to follow global rules and work for global community and actions. They have to research together to find areas for common work and cooperation.

It requires from countries to develop and accept the Global Constitutions, Legal Documents such as Global Trust Agreement.

As good example, there are long-lasting trends on a regional level, for example in EU, Eurasian Econom c Union and other regions.

On a global level, it will require to consider issues that are far beyond of the country's borders. For example, for Kazakhstan – it can be relationships with Africa, Latin America or Australia.

The difficulty of global politics is hidden in its way how countries can interact with each other without road, network or trade connections.

And here comes the wisdom of global politics – a global economics. What does it mean?

For example, on a global level, each country has its own competitive advantage. For example, in Kazakhstan we cannot produce banana so much like in sub or tropical countries. Or Brazil, has no competitive advantage than Kazakhstan in connecting Europe and Asia via land, or connecting Russia and Uzbekistan.

The next point is about understanding the main factors. There are several caterpillars of the global politics and they are:

- adoption of global constitution;

- acceptance of global rules;

- prioritizing global interest of all communities rather than local interests;

- building strategies for growing global citizens;

- understanding competitive advantage of the country in the global arena;

- defining the level of contribution of global citizens of the country for global economy;

- promoting the global education for global citizens;

- increasing a number of global citizens of the country;

- others;

Moreover, in the following table let us compare the main elements of national and global politics.

Table 1 Comparison of National and Global Politics

Priorities	National	Global
Country Programs	National, based on interest of limited groups, ethnical or tribal unions etc.	Global, based on interest including the interest of neighbor countries
Border policy	Closed, controlled, custom control zones	Open, crime control zones
Global Citizen Requirements	No, restricted	Yes, including global institutions for education, research, testing and issuing global citizen documentation or certification
Constitution	National, based on national values and traditions	Global, based on global values, issues and trends, including national advantages
Identity	Nationality, Ethnics, Social Status	Knowledge, Education, Citizenship
Currency policy	National currency, exchange	National and global currencies
Human rights	Respected to supporters and party	Respected to all, including minorities and global citizens
Market rules	The power of sellers, bankers and governors	The power of customer and consumers
Competitive Advantage	Access to finance and resources of limited groups, media coverage, territory or other elements	Education and science, R&D, transparency of wealth distribution, national economic competitiveness

		of geo-location and human resources
Values for Growth	Contacts, Tribal or Local Links and Connections, Corruption, Exceptional Random Contribution	Global Knowledge, Experience, Publications, Research, Purposeful Contribution, etc.

The table gives an understanding of how important to transform countries from national politics to global politics.

It includes many important priorities to consider to form a truly global environment that will support global citizens for greater contributions.

The table also includes the important elements of global economics, markets and other sectors, we have to uncover in the following sections.

Global Economics

In many sources, global economics tries to understand the global output, trade, export and import. It is our economic relations and it forms basic understanding of the global economics from national point of view.

But I believe when we talk about global economics, we have to understand the following elements first:

1) Global Population as a global human force;
2) Global Resources as a capacity for global growth;
3) Global Time as a man-hour measure and productivity;
4) Global Currency as a unit of income and expenditures of the global economy;
5) Global Output as a measure of global efficiency and growth.

For clearness, let me design the following comparison table.

Table 2 Comparison of National and Global Economics

Priorities	National Economics	Global Economics
Workforce	Priority to workforce with national skills	Priority to workforce with national and global skills
Time	Depends on cultural values	Valuable resource for global efficiency
Resources	National wealth	Source of global competitiveness and effectiveness
Currency	The symbol of national independence, payment	Source of saving, wealth, payment and investment
Trade: Export/Import	Source of national income and growth	Source of global competitive advantage
State Program	Improvement of National Competitiveness	Improvement of Global Competitive Advantage and Workforce

Ecological Issues	Within Border	Beyond Border
Legal Framework	National	Based on international values and best practices for fairness and human rights
Personal Information and Accounts	Vulnerable to State and Private Access and Infringements	Confidential to anybody, organization or person
Infrastructure	Exchange, Banks, Trade houses, Embassies, Governments	Global Platforms, Blockchain, E-commerce, Global Exchange, Global Payment Wallets

The table above provides ideas for deliberate process of decision making for global economics. In the context of the global economics, there many cornerstone priorities. Let's check the main elements out in detail.

Global Population and Time

At a global level, we divide population for many nationalities, boundaries, ethnic groups and so many other elements. And when it comes to global population, we cannot explain how we are going to solve global population issues in the mid and long term.

From my understanding, if we have 7 billion of citizens around the world, we know that there are 3,5 billion of workforce, who can work at different positions. They are the most powerful workforce of our planet. Among them, there are many who will be educated or illiterate. But we should understand the following arithmetic calculation for global efficiency.

Let's calculate the total number of work hours per day. If each person works 8 hours per day, the total sum of work hours is equal: 3,5 billion citizens * 8 hours/citizens = 28 billion hours per day.

For one year, it is around 10,22 trillion hours/year.

From global perspective, we can use this valuable time for anything that can make our world more efficient in many areas of global development. Imagine if every person will spend 1 hour a day for cleaning a planet. We will rid of from all waste in just one week.

For that we have to define the global work volume and the measurement of currency per hour. It is important that the payment scheme are fair, clear and in time.

Global Currency and Capital

Analyzing that we have a limited of hours per year, we can plan effectively the work amount and the volume of capital on a global scale. So, it will help to accelerate development and motivation of countries for new steps of progress.

If an average person will get USD 50 per hour, so the total volume of capital required for the global economy is USD 511 trillion.

So, it is understandable that if the GDP of the World Economy according to International Monetary Fund in 2019 is around USD 142 trillion, the rest of the capital will go for saving and investment of the future projects.

From a different angle, it shows that right now, each working person in the world (from 3,5 billion of workforce) is contributing on average for the World GDP with the amount of USD13,8 per working hour.

Generally, it shows that on the global level, there are many people, who work too much to produce the global wealth and there are many, who do not work at all. This shows that the global efficiency will be based on creation of the additional value by involving the unemployed part of the global workforce.

Global Resources

Our planet resources are limited and we do not know what consequences the planet can face because of extraction of natural resources from under the earth. We do not know how it will affect the circulation of our earth in the cosmos and generally for magnetic field or ozone shield of our planet.

Natural resources should be understood and evaluated not as resource for extraction but for their role for existence of our planet, balancing the earth's trajectory of movement around the sun and many other features.

These issues are out of the topic of the national governments and national organizations, which are focusing more on national interests of countries for 5-10 years at maximum. They do not care about how the planet will live in 50-100 years. What will be the conditions of climate and land for offspring and other living beings and for growing on the planet?

Without efforts of global institutions and global governance it is impossible to change the situation. The world needs some urgent actions for it. And I do not know now how long it will take to create a global government.

Global Government

Many organizations work on a global level to resolve the global issues. They are mainly financed by multinational companies or leading countries to solve their own issues.

The United Nations is one of the key structures for financing global projects too. But it again limited that it based on national interests and works on consequences.

On a global scale, we have also international financial institutions, international funds and unions such as European Union, which are financing many global projects for developing the regions. But again, the results of this organizations are difficult to evaluate and unseen. And most importunately, the policies are developed based on union's interests for long and midterm future.

Several years back I was developing a model of the global governance as one of the key experts of the Eurasian Economic Club of Scientists (see Figure below). It was thoughtful structure with many elements and relations to the present global institutions. That time cryptocurrencies were not in the media and the idea was to return to gold standard on a global level. But anyway, it was not interesting to any of the governors as it required some efforts to unite nations.

Even though the idea of the structure is still demanding and for implementation of such a global scale project we need more powerful institution which can control the global governance and currency volume.

It was 5 years back. Now we see the rise of cryptocurrencies and at the same time the active position of such institutions such as Global Citizen, G-Global International Secretariat and many other global organizations.

And as an outcome, there is a question, what kind of global government we need now.

Global Government should be based on the following:

1) Legitimacy of the country;
2) Adoption of the global constitution;
3) Acceptance of global currencies;
4) Respect of national boundaries and cultures;
5) Creation of the global parliament;
6) Development of the global bank and payment system etc.

These are not the easy tasks, but it will help to create an infrastructure for growth of global citizens in any country of the world.

There are many sceptics and opponents of the global government, in fact. It is understandable that countries want to have more power and control their resources and capital by their own. In fact, even today, national governments are focused only on benefits of the target activities for their countries.

When we talk about the global marketplace, global government is more an issue of the global communities to take an active role in realizations of global actions.

Figure 1 Mechanisms of Development of New World Financial System and the New World Currency

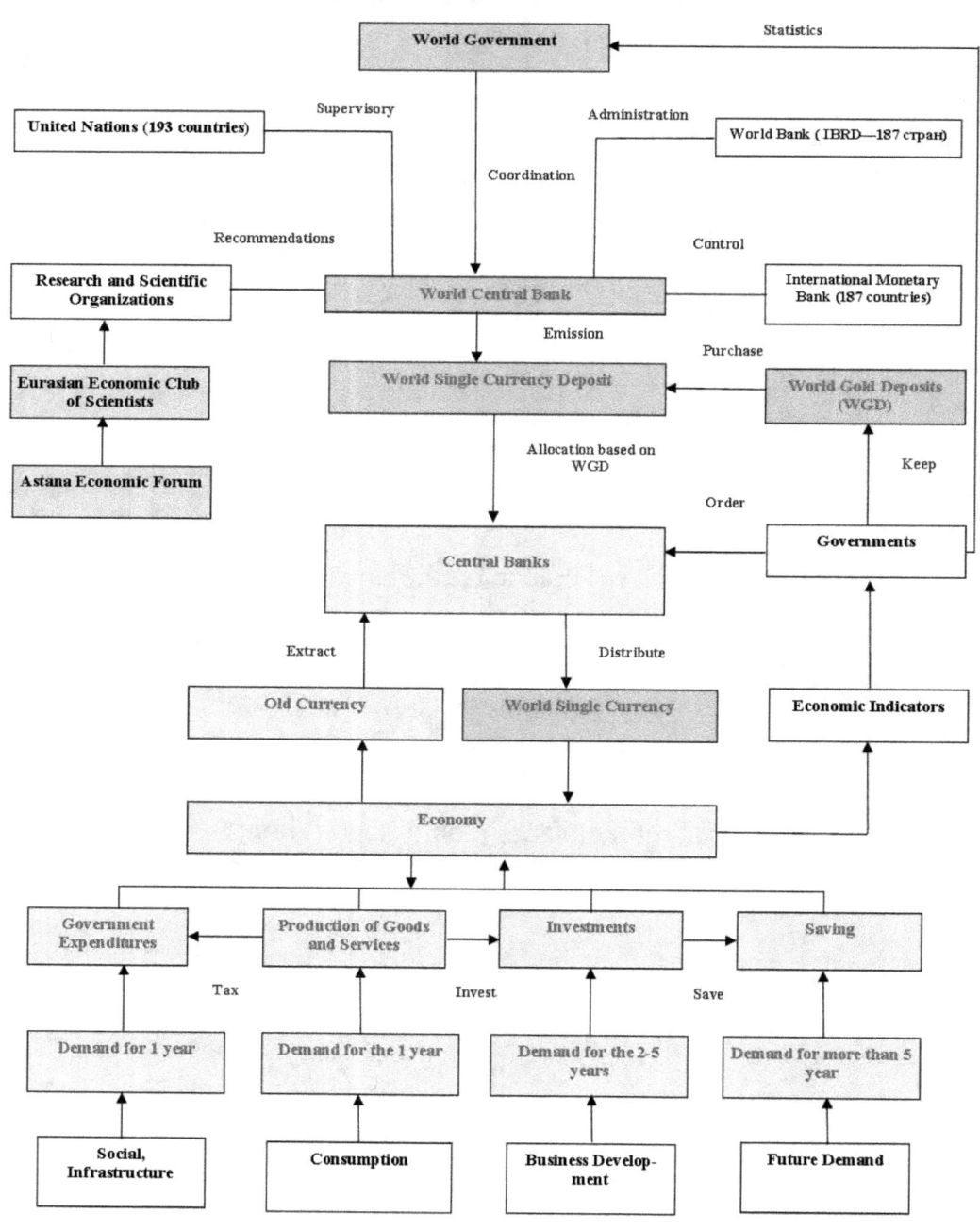

PROPOSAL OF EURASIAN ECONOMIC CLUB OF SCIENTISTS
IN THE V ASTANA ECONOMIC FORUM

MECHANISMS OF DEVELOPMENT OF NEW WORLD FINANCIAL SYSTEM
AND THE NEW WORLD CURRENCY

From practical point, we see that global institutions, businesses and international organizations are ready to cooperate to improve the situation in the certain country with limited focus on cross-national projects. They also are ready only on those projects, which has the guaranteed financial mechanism for realization of the actions from the local governments. Of course, with such kind of approach, we cannot resolve and clean fully our oceans, for example, which has no owners or government to control.

In addition, we cannot accept the fact that each citizen of any country has to pay the global tax in order to accumulate the funds of the global government. Moreover, governments do not want to pay additional contribution when they pay for membership in the United Nations' Organizations and many other international organizations.

So, it is not simple to build a global government in one year. There are many barriers and issues which decrease the legitimacy of the global government in practice. Especially without financial system.

So, I was thinking that global government can start on a virtual global environment, developed with the purpose to bring volunteer citizens – global citizens for contributing and creating in the electronic environment.

E-Global Government

E-Global Government can be an initial stage of the creating Global Government in practice.

Global Citizens can join from any place where they have internet access. And E-Global Government can be a place where Global Citizens can join under special terms and rules to act and support global actions, create their own cryptocurrency for supporting their actions or take the existing cryptocurrencies. They can also elect their E-Global Parliament and E-Global Government providing certain quotes for countries and rotating their leaders in the positions in the E-Global Parliament and E-Global Government.

To make the system of E-Global Government working, the requirements can be based on government and international experiences of unions. For example, in order to become a member of the E-Global Government, for each specific position there should be a vote system based on quote for each country.

In addition, member and interested governments can create a budget on the blockchain with specific purpose to finance the projects of the E-Global Government on a global scale, where any member or global citizen can take part as a specialist, volunteer or intern.

In other words, E-Global Government will work as a system, which unite the functionalities of such systems as Facebook, Cryptocurrency Wallets and E-Gov Platforms of many countries.

This platform will help to bring new type of citizens – Global Citizens, who can contribute effectively for the development of their countries and the global economy.

The important part is a global infrastructure, which should serve effectively the system and defend global citizens from any prejudices, local manipulations, corruptions etc.

Global Infrastructure

Global Infrastructure should save time, effectively allocate global resources or unite global citizens in the projects and at the same time defend them from any violation of their rights and principles.

We have to understand that the infrastructure is dependent on many other areas such as Transport, Engineering, Geography, IT, Communication, Legal System, Human Rights, Budgeting, Food Security, Ecology, Quality Management, Global Supply Chain Management, Global Governance and many others.

Globally, the topic is more discussed in the context of global and international businesses, but in the context of global infrastructure for global citizens there is no information and the appropriate infrastructure is only discussed in the context of global tourism infrastructure.

Therefore, I would like to focus on several key concepts to draw the main points of the global infrastructure development.

Global Food Security

According to many international sources, there are more than 2 billion people live in poverty and hunger. It is around 30% of the world population.

Figure 2 Roadmap for Ensuring Food Security

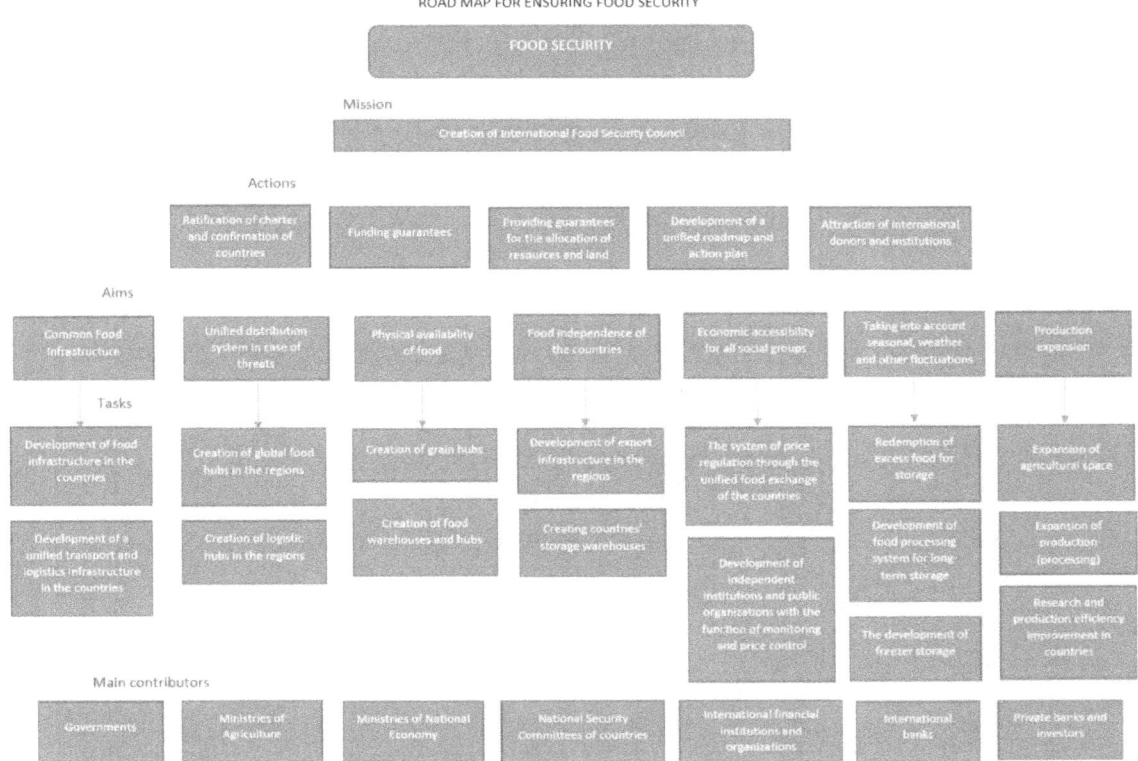

Several years ago, I had a chance to prepare a strategic roadmap for food security and placed in many sources.

The figure of the section is an outcome of discussions and brainstorming about global food security where we can see a complex mechanism for global food security infrastructure.

Realization of such project requires a lot of efforts for agreeing many details with every country and it takes years for looking for investments.

As I showed this concept and shared it in Kazakhstan, the country has the key advantage to focus on its food security infrastructure and network. On a country level, it was quite fast to start the preliminary steps for implementation.

Even though it was slow, but in all regional centers of Kazakhstan, now we have warehouses and food stability funds. It helps local people access high quality and fresh products, including vegetables and fruits.

I hope this concept can move the global food security infrastructure and help global community to create stability funds and infrastructure in the period of global climate changes.

To realize a global infrastructure for global citizens, it is important to develop a concept or roadmap for local governments that can support the idea on a country level first.

Based on analysis and design of the systems of several countries, in my book "Waste Management: From Concept to Action Plan" I described many models for waste management.

Without this concept, it was not easy to explain to many green leaders of the country before I wrote this book. And when it was launched, I placed it in the internet forums of the Astana Economic Forum and other platforms to discuss it with experts.

Figure 3 Example of Formation of HIW by Consumer

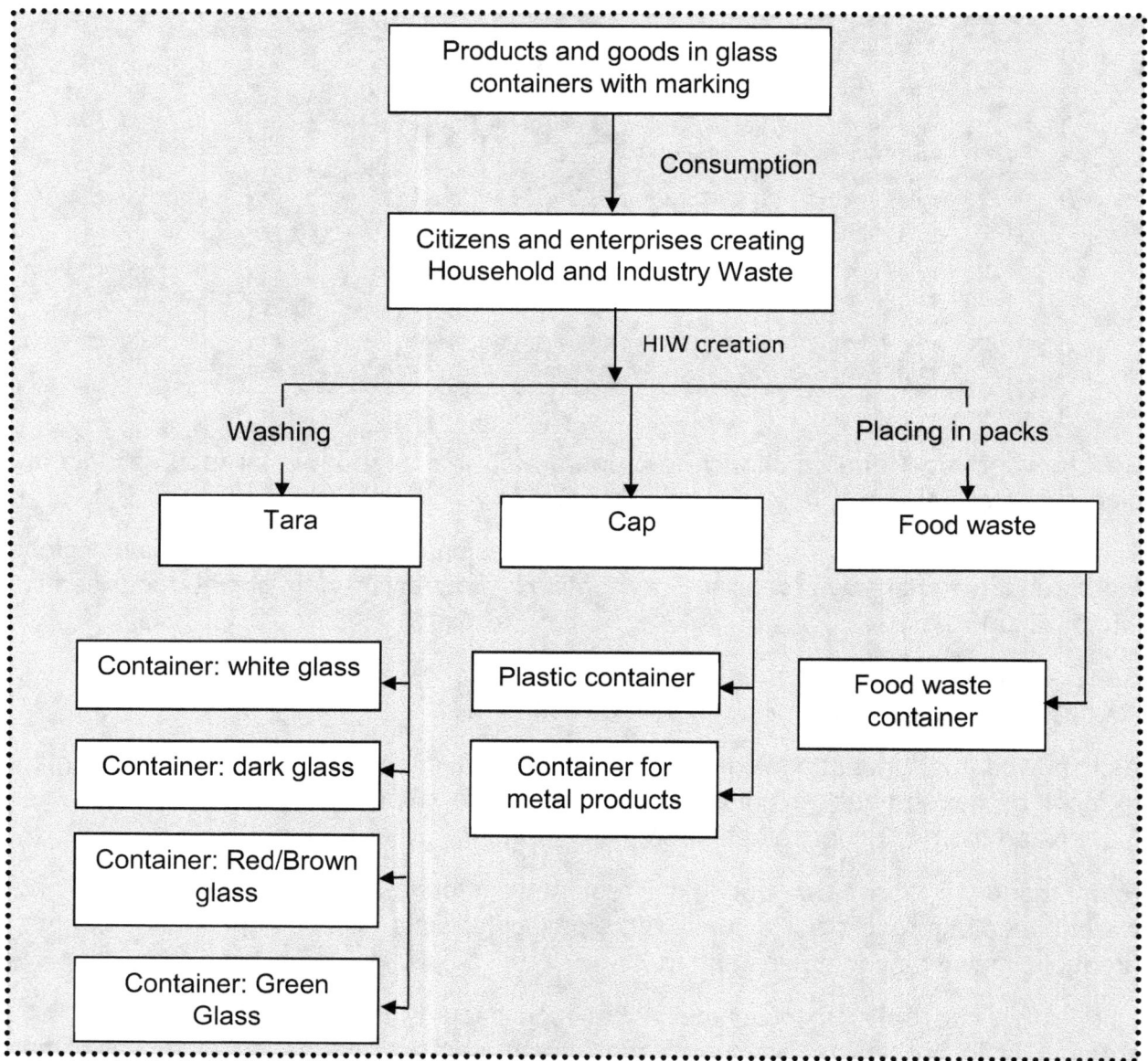

It does not work to fast, as many points of the concept were far from understanding. And without understanding waste business, it is impossible to attract the investor.

Even the idea was clear and I saw some progress in increasing the audience, investors were reluctant to join the waste business. As locally, waste was something disgusting and associated with something dirty and smelly. It was hard to broke the stereotypes of local mind. And required some time and another angle to start with.

Generally, an ideal waste management system is a complex infrastructure, which can be launched only with global mind. The figure 3 is one of the examples of formation of waste by consumers.

When we take waste, from regional point of view, there are some boundaries which limit countries to stop their financing of the ecology and waste projects. That is because of budget deficit. Therefore, in many countries, including in Central Asia, ecology and waste issues are getting their solutions very slowly.

Moreover, corruption and absence of standards become a main barrier for protecting the environmental programs. Let's take an example in automotive industry. Today, many countries of the Central Asia became a market of used cars with the lowest ecological standards. Millions of such cars on the roads are polluting environments without any legal requirements for ecological standards.

When we take into account the global infrastructure for ecology and waste, we have to understand that it requires building infrastructure gradually. It is not possible to build a 100% zero waste infrastructure in one year or even 5 years. As it requires a strong educational and research institutions for constant information policies and trainings of population including from kindergarten children to up to old people, who handle waste every day.

Global Rights

Global Human Rights are the sensitive topic for many economies, especially with authoritarian, religious and dictatorship systems.

In many countries to protect the human rights, the following institutions are working:

1) Lawyers;
2) Judges;
3) Public institutions;
4) NGOs;
5) Ombudsman.

But on a regional and country level they are all dependent on government decisions and budgets. So, if the person really needs support about his violated human rights by government, there is no way that these institutions will protect the citizens.

On international level, the following communities are playing an important role:

1) Social Networks including Facebook, Instagram;
2) International Amnesty Organization;
3) United Nations Human Rights Organization;

4) International Lawyers;

5) International Organizations etc.

Nowadays, for example, Facebook and International Amnesty Organization are much stronger institutions to protect the human rights of individuals in any country.

Global Citizens are one of the key citizens to whom not only the global infrastructure should work properly, but also, they are the key players of building global infrastructure for other citizens of our planet.

Only Global Citizens can provide right and appropriate solutions or actions for building a global infrastructure for waste and ecology management, protection of human rights or providing food security around the world.

It depends on many issues and factors, but the most important factor is a global culture of the Global Citizens. This factor will form true Global Citizens with strong ideology for global action around the world.

Global Culture

Global Citizen is a person with strong ideological position for development of global communities by common actions.

Only Global Culture will be an indicator of the values and character of the Global Citizen and exemplary for other citizens. Via Global Culture, national citizens can understand the high values and mission of the Global Citizens and try to support them and also join one day their row.

The global culture can be discussed from many points, but one of the key elements are the following.

Citizenship

Global Citizenship is a legal prove of the Global Citizen. It can be in the form of the passport or identification document from Global Government or Global Institutions which can independently evaluate the contribution of the national citizens and issue an identification document.

Global Citizenship should be a legal document that can protect the rights of global citizens, open access to countries for greater contribution and actions and allow receiving benefits from global activities.

It is not clear who can issue this document or where it can be taken. But there should be some legal institution or government supported by members of world countries or global institutions.

Another good experience has Estonia, where they started to issue e-residency to any person from around the world several years ago. It can be in the same format for Global

Citizenship in case of difficulty for creating a legal institution for issuing paper identification.

History

There were a lot of cases in the history which can remote countries from global unity. For examples, in many countries of the post-soviet system, many ethnic groups do not like Russians or Chinese people because of their negative historical actions in the past, especially for mass killings and deportation of noble families.

The same to Iranians or North Koreans, who have absolutely outdated thinking about global issues and see the United States as a danger for their stability.

Historically, Iranians think that they are the only country where they link themselves to the prophet of the Mahomed. It is still preserved and they do not want to see Americans, British, French, Jews who they believe are the main enemy for Islam in the region.

But they totally do not understand that many Muslim diaspores are living in the US, UK, France and other countries of the world, including Islamic Banks which are first originated in the UK.

Global Citizens should know not only the details of global history, but also a reality of global new history for global diversity and development.

It is impossible to live with single ideology for progress. If there will be no competitive ideologies there will be no rescue balloon from global tyranny.

One of the key points of the global history is the acceptance of the same ancestors. Today we have genetical analysis and some cultures preserved their tribal trees, which link one nationality to many cultures of the world.

It is important for the unity of the nations to include a genetic test information in to the global identification document and create a new history of Global Citizens.

Values

Many cultures and nationalities have the same values, traditions and religions. They coexist as neighbor countries, but many divided by political control of the leading nations of the past.

For example, many Central Asian or Middle East countries has the same historical leaders and therefore have the same values, attitudes and relationships in cultures.

For example, ethnic groups of Kazakhstan, Uzbekistan, Kyrgyzstan, Tajikistan and Turkmenistan have the same national hero Alpamys. Many families read the tales of Alpamys to their children to grow them strong in faith and power, patriotic and gentlemen.

However, these countries have their new political systems with their own government and borders. And for global citizens it is a way to approach to countries with the same values despite the differences in dialects and languages.

The same can be found on the global level. For example, many people red or saw Charles Dicken's stories or Peter Jackson's fantasy adventure film "The Lord of Rings". These are the films which formed many values of people, including todays of etiquette in many spheres.

For Global Citizens it is important to drive the nations for new actions via understanding their values and building new global values.

What the main global values today. Let's list them:

1) Honesty;
2) Fairness;
3) Goodwill;
4) Faithfulness;
5) Openness;
6) Love of freedom;
7) Respect for Equality;
8) Supportiveness;
9) Adventurous;
10) Respect of superiority of the knowledge;
11) Generosity;
12) Global mindset;
13) Others.

Global Citizen has to understand all the values of the character and try promote them in other people.

Traditions

Only in Kazakhstan we have 100 of traditions which are specific only for the country. And there are also regionally traditions, which are specific only for the regions.

The idea of the book is to create many new global traditions for global unity, exchange, communication and development.

When we talk about global traditions, it should include the following traditions:

1) Debates;
2) Discussions;
3) Forums;
4) Brainstorming;
5) Contests;
6) Polls;
7) Feedbacks;
8) Meetings of various types;
9) Demonstrations;
10) Presentations;
11) How to do activities;

12)Investor Days;
13)Field workshops;
14)Parties;
15)Concerts;
16)Shows;
17)Interviews;
18)Actions;
19)Etc.

Global Traditions should allow global citizens effectively communicate, interact and exchange with like-minded global and national citizens and also old-minded or persons limited in their border area. Traditions of global citizens should help to better understand each other and build truly global communities.

Religion

There are more than 100 religions around the world, and there are around 4 main streams. From global understanding, we have to have a global religion with new values and belief of the power of the God in absolutely new meaning and practices.

They should include the following new meaning and practices:

1) Reading of books with critical view and opportunities for new ideas;
2) Keep the appropriate rules and practices of main religions;
3) Start the actions and thanks God in any global action, including in eating and sleeping;
4) Use effectively water, resources and knowledge;
5) Help poorer and socially vulnerable people;
6) Promote global values, traditions, thinking and religion;
7) Defend the human rights, including of women and children;
8) Work, act, learn and teach with passion for development global values;
9) Keep loyalty for global principles, values, traditions and religion;
10) Stand strong for any ideas and offers against wars, corruption and other negative actions against humanity, nature and peace;
11) Unite people for global religion of new deeds and actions;
12) Open and create future opportunities for all.

New global religion is not about praying and individual or group practices in the interest of religious groups, but rather it is a new way of thinking in the interest of good faith and future.

Thinking and Ideology

Global Culture is a new global thinking approach and a new element of global ideology. It is impossible to implement the global culture without them.

Global Thinking is all about how global citizens think in different situations, especially in critical one.

For example, in case of sudden war between countries, it is important for global citizens to protect the fairness and the rights of humans who have no relations to war parties.

Global ideology is based on the level of knowledge, experience and actions about the global environment, culture and politics. The ideology is stronger in the people, who has wider knowledge of the global history, politics, culture etc.

And global ideology is one of the strongest tools for building an appropriate global thinking in global citizens.

To expand the global thinking and ideology in other communities and people, it is important to focus on global presence. It is about how the ideas are transferred to masses to help them understand the global thinking and ideology for all.

Global Presence

There are many ways for global presence for a global citizen. In my book "200 web-sites and tools for online presence: essential handbook for marketing and growth" I classified 200 web-sites and tools, which should help anyone to succeed in online presence. An approach of the book from business point can be also applicable for the global activities.

For a global citizen, it is important to do necessary steps for describing the processes and activities for global communities. This is a new way how other national citizens can be motivated and build interest for global actions.

Time and Mobility

Time is the most valuable resource for global citizens. It is important to understand the available time on a global scale for global actions.

At the same time, global mobility is a key element to involve global citizens in very urgent cases. For example, a global citizen of Kazakhstan with the vast experience in development of the country can move to another location, where a citizen can easily contribute for the development of any other developing country in Asia, Middle East, Africa, Central or South America.

Mobility of global citizens will create the best opportunities for global presence.

Communication

Global Presence requires very strong communication skills and it is important to talk and speak to other people and connect effectively them with each other for common actions. In other words, for teambuilding.

Therefore, it is not only about language or verbal skills, but also about negotiation, cultural, religious and NLP skills which are important to understand the decision-making processes of various cultural and ethnical groups.

Global citizens can improve communication skills only through communication and interaction both on professional level and everyday level, including in building relationships for cooperation and achieving the same missions.

Global Actions

As a global citizen with strong ideology for global development it is time for global actions.

There are several ways to start global actions without any resources or capital. The only requirement is a patience and consistent work on achieving the progress for global thinking.

Generally, the main requirements for global actions are:

-set a mission for global actions, for example, to change my region and make it first on the global map for new achievements;

-develop positive attitude to achieve the mission;

-plan your global actions for each action with clear outcomes for the region, people and yourself;

-meet and communicate with people uniting them for global actions;

-implement global actions with leadership and responsibility about your region, people and offspring;

-present your ideas and mission clearly, receive feedback from team and audiences;

-evaluate your implemented global actions to make the next action more resultative.

These standard requirements to follow the process. But it is also important to focus on content and personal skills.

The most influential instruments and tools for global actions are:

-interesting and constant content;

-real facts from around the world;

-good speaking and presentation skills;

-audience involvement with feedback, polls Q&A and interactions;

-statistics and comparisons of data;

-offering new ideas and projects for common action and others.

After meeting your audiences, they have to feel that they will act differently and they will change their principles for that.

Note that in many regions, people need more meetings to get the meaning for change. And the global citizen has to plan a long-term action plan.

As a fact, well-known that person remembers only 30% of information in 1 hour after the presentation. In one day only 10% of it. And it requires 18-20 times to see the content to remember it for a life. Therefore, the content of the global citizen should be:

1) Impressive;
2) Easy to remember;
3) Easy to imagine;
4) Easy to read and understand;
5) Accessible at any time via internet

A global citizen should also understand that some content has to be presented 18-20 times, not in one year, but maybe in 5-10 years, depending on the complexity of the topic for global change.

Many times, global citizens will be not understood by surrounding people. Because they act without financial support and interest in it to achieve the mission. Only the achieving a mission can help the Global Citizen to find a way to sources of funding and investment.

At the same time, a global citizen should understand at least 40-50 alternative sources of income to support his global actions on a constant base without financial resources or support.

The final point is how to cope with resistance from public or government officials. Many global actions will become a barrier for individuals and government officials to earn money from corrupted schemes or policies. They will show great resistance in many ways to destroy the plans of the global citizens. They will try to involve public, youth and socially vulnerable groups of people to show their resistance.

Therefore, for global actions it is important to consider targeted information strategies in various information channels and groups.

Mission for Regional Change

Here in this section, I would like to show an example of contribution for global change in one of the regions of Kazakhstan in year 2018.

My missions for regional development started from the point to change the region and demonstrate its competitive advantages on a global arena.

For achieving a mission, I decided to involve international experts from one side, and called for actions in many areas of international and regional collaboration, cooperation and activities.

Let me provide you with photo examples and how this helped to expand the horizons of local people.

17.01.2018 Organization of meetings and participation in the Kazakh-Portuguese Business Forum, Almaty city

Organizing meetings with representatives of Portugal helped to see and evaluate the region's level development in construction, agriculture, including in meat processing and greenhouse productivity.

25.01.2018 Meeting with an entrepreneur in Shymkent to attract investment, RIC "Ontustik"

Meeting local businessmen and discussing various types of projects helped to motivate local businesses for global markets and development of tourism infrastructure.

06.03.2018 Meeting on the project development with youth, RIC "Ontustik"

Cooperation with the most active youth of the region helped the regional investment center and generally the government to see the main problems of youth, especially those with global education.

15.03.2018 Business Meeting on the export of strawberries and other berries, RIC "Ontustik" with the Director of the Procurement Company from Russia

Bringing business procurement director and farmers in one table meeting, which provided many ideas for developing agricultural sector of the region. It also helped us to evaluate the main problems of agriculture compared to Turkey, Russia, Uzbekistan and other Middle East countries.

17.03.2018 Organization of commodity exhibition for local producers and farmers, RIC "Ontustik"

04.03.2018 Participation in the meeting with FoodSIB Company to export products, Government of South-Kazakhstan region

20-30 март 2018 Presentations on the development of export potential in 16 districts and cities of South Kazakhstan Region

9-11 April 2018 Promotion in the region the Annual Investment Meeting in Dubai: www.aimcongress.com

16.04.2018 Participation in Invest Day and meeting with Raev N., a private investor from Astana, and young entrepreneurs, Chaplin Café

17.05.2018 Participation in the XI Astana Economic Forum with the participation of the Head of State, Astana-EXPO, Astana city

22.05.2018 the Business Forum of Kazakhstan and Uzbekistan,
Meetings with leaders of international organizations, Zoodel and KazakhExport, Rixos Hotel
Khadisha, Shymkent City

19.05.2018 Round table on the development of a green economy in the South Kazakhstan
region, M.Auezov South-Kazakhstan State University, Shymkent City

20.05.2018 Organization of Meeting for South-Korean Delegation with Akim and Deputy Akim of Turkestan city, Turkestan City

Meeting with an export manufacturer of safflower oil, Shymkent City

25.05.2018 Meeting with prof. Kim Kwang Don, South-Kazakhstan State University

05.06.2018 Organization of Meeting between Deputy Akim of Shymkent Baymakhanov Timur Sultanbekovich and Kim Kwang Don, Korean Expert in Construction and Concreate

07.06.2018 Meeting with the Executive Director of the International Science and Technology Center David Cleave in Astana

07.06.2018 Meeting with the head of the International Center for Green Technologies and Investment Projects Zhoshybayev Rapil Seythanovich in Astana city

09.06.2018 Meeting with ASTANA Innovations' Chairman of the Board Mr. Olzhas Sartayev, Astana City

07.06.2018~09.06.2018 Organization of the visit of the delegation from region to the Summit Forum on Renewable Energy in Astana city

12.06.2018 Meeting with Deputy Akim of Shymkent Baymahanov Timur Sultanbekovich

14.06.2018 Presentation on the topic of Shymkent Development to the directors of departments of the Government of Shymkent City

28.06.2018 Memorandum signed between SKSU, RTC "Ontustik" and the Association for Ecological Organizations

28.06.2018 Organizing Meeting of the Director General of the Department of International Cooperation of the Korea Environment Corporation Yu Jeyhon and Professor Rae Kwon Chung with the Akim of the Turkestan Region Zhanseit Tyuimebayev

28.06.2018 Organizing Meeting with Director General of the Department of International Cooperation of the Korea Environment Corporation Yu Jeyhon and Professor Rae Kwon Chung with Shymkent Akim of Gabidulla Abdrahimov and at Shymkent Agrarian College

01.07.2018~03.07.2018 Organizing Meeting for Deputy Chairman of RIC "Ontustik" within the Forum of Mayors of Cities of the Silk Road countries - GLOBAL SILK ROAD in Astana city

01.07.2018~03.07.2018 Organizing Meeting for Deputy Chairman of RIC "Ontustik" within the Forum of Mayors of Cities of the Silk Road countries - GLOBAL SILK ROAD in Astana city

10.07.2018 Organizing Meeting with participation of «JV Robo Avia» and SKSU

13.07.2018 Organizing Meeting between representatives of Department of Architecture of the Shymkent Government and the Korean company HEERIM

17.07.2018 Appointed as an Advisor to Shymkent Agrarian College, Turkestan Higher Agrarian College

20.07.2018~23.07.2018 Evaluating Laboratories of South-Kazakhstan State University

30.07.2018 Memorandum signed between SKSU and Korean Concrete Institute, South-Kazakhstan State University

30.07.2018 Memorandum was signed between SKSU, RIC "Ontustik" and the Korean Concrete Institute, South-Kazakhstan State University

30.07.2018 Memorandum signed between SKSU, RIC "Ontustik" and LLP "JV RoboAvia", South-Kazakhstan State University

30.07.2018 Organizing Meeting of the delegation from KCI with the Chairman of the Board of the RIC "Ontustik" Baytore Kuanysh

30.07.2018 Organizing Meeting of the delegation from the KCI with the Deputy Akim of Shymkent Bauyrzhan Mamytaliev

September - till present, Participation in the development of www.mep.kz, a project for the export development office of the Akimat of Turkestan region

08.08.2018 Organizing Meeting with prof. Kim Kwang Don in the RIC "Ontustik"

23.08.2018~25.08.2018 Organizing Meetings about the investment projects and for signing a memorandum between SKSU, RIC "Ontustik", SHINSUNG E&G and "ON EXPORT" LLP

24.08.2018 Organizing Tour for participation in Melonfest in Zhetysay city

12.09.2018 Organizing Meeting at the Research and Production Center for grain farming in the Nauchniy

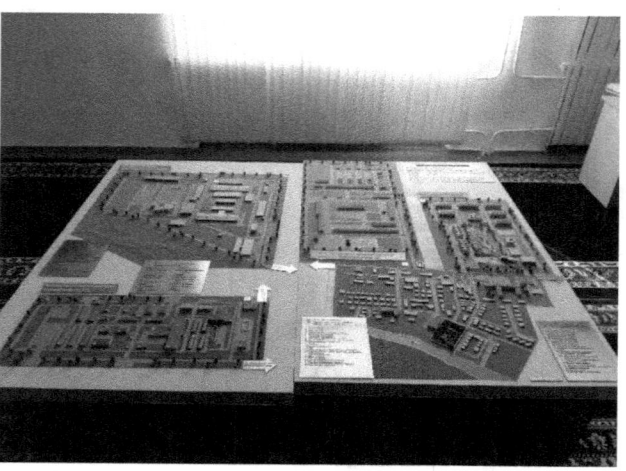

18.09.2018 Organizing Lecture in Shymkent Agrarian College on the topic: Innovative activity of ShAC through innovation, export and competitiveness of the agricultural sector of the region and Shymkent city

Since September 2018, teaching in SKSU topics: Competitiveness and Management, Project Management and Marketing Communication

18.09.2018 Organizing Meeting on the implementation of the rector's orders in SKSU M.Auezova

12.11.2018 Organizing Presentation of projects in Agrocollege of Turkestan region

12.11.2018 Handing the certificates for the best project initiators of the Agrocollege of Turkestan region

10.11.2018 Collaboration in Days of France in Kazakhstan, Rixos Hotel

15.11.2018 Organization of the presentation of students of SKSU in the RIC "Ontustik"

28.11.2018 Organization and participation in the V International Conference of Engineering and Technology, South-Kazakhstan State University

29.11.2018 Organization of a Meeting with engineers from South Korea, Kazavtodor LLP

30.11.2018 Participation in the round table on the topic of Mustafa Chokai

08.12.2018 Participation in the Shymkent Development Forum, Rixos Hotel

25.12.2018 Organization and participation in the Agriculture Conference, South-Kazakhstan State University

Conclusion

Growing global citizens requires many efforts and areas to develop.

We have to understand that this is not a one-year process or activity, rather it is a constant work and long-term actions.

I hope that for readers this book showed many corners to work on the main issues for building and growing a number of global citizens in the country. And I hope that my children will understand the work of his farther and about why he was so busy with a book many nights without attention to them.

While writing I could also see many areas and directions, where I can focus on writing of a new book near future and it provided me with an idea to continue my doctoral degree on one of the key issues of the global agenda.

I call my readers and many interested citizens with global mindset for cooperation and collaboration for research and development of new tools and solutions for global citizenship.

Feel free to contact me for your ideas and comments via email at nurbek2020@gmail.com

About author

Nurbek Achilov is a global citizen with more than 20 years of experience in international activities, forums and events. He holds a Visionary Level on Global Citizen Platform with his over 100 global actions to support global leaders.

He is involved as a lecturer of marketing and management at the South-Kazakhstan State University where he focuses on preparation of students with global orientations in marketing, management and other disciplines.

Nurbek is a founder of several organizations and projects in several countries. He enjoys writing about multiple issues of the global economy and development. As a member of educational institutions, he understands well about the problems of global economy and development. He explores many areas on how to improve the situation to help the regions to adapt to the international level.

Where can you find interesting stories about investments, export and trade on the internet?

Nurbek Achilov has some resources for you!

On Blogger's platform he runs his blog about investments, export, trade and other issues.

Blog about investment, export and trade in English:

https://nurbekachilov.blogspot.com/

Blog about investment, export and trade in English:

https://nurbekachil.blogspot.com/

You can also find ideas, photos and experiences about investments, trade and investment on Nurbek Achilov's pages in Facebook, Instagram, Pinterest, Slideshare,

Academia and LinkedIn and other accounts.

orcid.org/0000-0003-1238-6556

Kazakhstan

Tips for Travelers

Nurbek Achilov

Second Edition

2019

Get my new book with the Special Price on Amazon.com

200 web-sites and tools for online presence

Essential Handbook for marketing and growth

Nurbek Achilov

First Edition

2019

Waste Management

From Concept till Action Plan

Nurbek Achilov

First Edition

2010